BRITAIN'S
SECOND
D-DAY

Decimalisation 1971

STEWART BINNS

INTRODUCTION

With not a little trepidation, Britain stepped into the brave new world of decimal currency in February 1971. After a rather unsettled end of January, the weather for the first two weeks of the month was dominated by high pressure. This brought lots of sunny weather, but without the cooler temperatures usually associated with winter high pressure.

Monday 15th February, decimal day itself, saw the weather break. Four millimetres of rain fell on the 15th, the first for a fortnight, leading many cynics to suggest that it was an omen that the discarding of one of the country's oldest and most precious traditions was not an auspicious move. There was a little more rain the following day, but then settled weather returned, only confirming the doomsayers' conviction that the gods of Britain's ancient heritage were not best pleased with the arrival of an 'alien' monetary system.

Fifty years have now passed, and Britain's old imperial coinage system has become a thing of curious amusement for most people. Although recollections of 'thrupenny bits', 'tanners' and 'florins' provoke wry smiles from younger generations, I am old enough to remember with fondness the passing of old friends in our pockets and purses. I also have a very clear memory of the day itself.

Opposite: The new decimal fifty pence was the world's first seven sided coin when it was first released in 1969

3

Even your morning coffee could come with a ready reckoner for converting predecimal to decimal currency

ISBN: 978-1-63972-091-0
Published by Inspire Creative, PO Box 59, Axminster EX13 9AH.

I was a final-year undergraduate at university and my morning ritual was a relaxed start with the purchase of a newspaper and a bottle of Coca Cola from the campus newsagent. I knew it was decimal day. It was impossible not to know; for weeks beforehand, the publicity, speculation and controversy had dominated the news.

So, it was with a mix of emotions, curiosity and anticipation, that I watched the shopkeeper open his till to take my '50 new penny piece', which had been introduced in 1969 by the Decimal Currency Board to pave the way for decimalisation. And there they were, a gleaming set of bright new copper coins: the new halfpenny, penny and two pence (the new five pence and ten pence silver coins had both been introduced in 1968 as part of the transition process).

My Guardian newspaper cost 6d (imperial price), 2½p in 'new' money, and my Coke 7d (imperial price) 3p in 'new' money, making a total of 5½p to pay. So, the shopkeeper, with a quick glance at one of the numerous crib sheets that had been printed for the transition, handed me my change from my seven-sided 50 pence piece: a handful of new coins, both silver and copper, totalling 44½p. There in my hand were four 10p coins, four 1p coins, and one ½p coin. Why did I pay with such a high denomination coin and thus receive so much change? There were two reasons: I wanted to see the new coins, but, more truthfully, like so many people, I had no idea how to do the arithmetic of transition, so gave him 50p to be safe!

THE ROAD TO D-DAY

Although China had been using a decimal system for at least two millennia, Russia's ruble was the first decimalised currency to be used in Europe when it was introduced in 1704 by Russia's most important reformer, Peter the Great. Similarly, instigated by America's great reformer, Thomas Jefferson, President George Washington's Coinage Act of 1792 introduced decimal currency to the United States, the first English speaking country to adopt a decimalised coinage system.

The most significant path to modern decimal and metric systems began in France when its people were engaged in changes much more profound than innovations in counting, measurement and currency. In 1790, Charles-Maurice de Talleyrand-Périgord, the wily and gifted diplomat, who would survive the Ancien Régime, the Revolution and Napoleon, carried a resolution in the National Assembly which suggested the adoption of a scientific standard by all nations.

In order to derive a symbolic base for measurement, Talleyrand proposed, "That a commission be formed charged

Opposite: The new decimal ten pence was first released in 1968, more than two years before changeover, and was the same size and value as the predecimal florin, to allow people to become accustomed to the new coins and their values.

with the duty of ascertaining the length of the pendulum beating seconds in latitude 45°." Eventually, in 1793, a 'metre', from the Greek, 'metron' (a measure) became the base unit of length in the International System of Units and was determined to be one ten-millionth of the distance from the equator to the North Pole along a great circle.

Eventually, Talleyrand's resolution led to the introduction of a uniform decimal coinage and the metrication of international weights and measures. The old 'livre' was replaced by the 'franc', part of a grand scheme to metricise everything, including weights, measures, dates and even time.

In 1793, the French, believing that the calendar and even time were based on logic derived from archaic religion and oppressive aristocratic power decided that standard time should be abolished in favour of 'French Revolutionary Time', which would have a 10-hour day, with 100 minutes per hour, and 100 seconds per minute. The new system did have a few practical benefits, particularly in simplifying how to calculate time-based arithmetic. For example, if you could get over midday being 5 o'clock it became relatively easy to work out that 65% of a day would be 6 hours and 50 minutes, rather than 15:36. French Revolutionary Time was both an elegant and simple alternative. Unfortunately, traditional 24-hour time, based on a methodology devised by the Ancient Egyptians, had been used for millennia and old habits die hard.

French Revolutionary Time officially began on November 24th, 1793 although conceptual work around the system had been going on for over 40 years. The French manufactured clocks and watches showing both decimal time and standard time on their faces, which only added to the confusion...and mistrust.

The revolutionary system was unpopular because, except for mathematicians there was no real reason for ordinary 18th century French people, who used the sun as a time-piece, to change how they told the time. Moreover, replacing every clock and watch in the country was a very expensive undertaking. On the other hand, the metric system of weights and measurements, which helped standardise commerce, did have a significant simplicity, even for ordinary French peasants and workers.

The French abandoned the use of decimal time after just 17 months, when French Revolutionary Time became non-mandatory starting on 7th April 1795. Even so, some areas of the country continued to observe decimal time, and a few decimal clocks remained in use for years afterwards. The French tried again in 1897, when the 'Commission de décimalisation du temps proposed a 24-hour day with 100-minute hours, again with 100 seconds per minute. The proposal was scrapped in 1900. Interestingly, it is still possible to find original French decimal clocks and pocket watches, but they are very rare and prohibitively expensive.

Through a commission from the patrons of the Tate Gallery, visual artist, Ruth Ewan, produced ten decimal clocks for Folkestone's Triennial in 2011 called, 'We Could Have Been Anything We Wanted To Be'. All the clocks were displayed publicly, some in very prominent positions such as on the town hall facade, and others that had to be either searched for or happened upon by chance, such as those found in a pub or a local taxi. With each clock, Ewan replaced the dials and mechanism to achieve the decimal regulation of time.

Despite the failure of some of France's more radical innovations, the long journey to the world's decimal/metricated future had begun. In 1817 the Netherlands decimalised, followed in 1855 by Sweden, the Austro-Hungarian Empire in 1857, Japan in 1868 and the German Empire in 1873.

In Britain, the issue of decimalised currency had been discussed since at least 1682, when economist, Sir William Petty, a friend of Samuel Pepys, proposed a system, 'to keep all Accompts in a way of Decimal Arithmetick'. However, in Britain, ingrained tradition and political intransigence and weakness prevented innovation and change. Britain felt that it was above adopting a 'gimmick' from Europe and the United States, a former colony, of course.

The looming figure of Napoleon, and his conquests in Europe, was also a factor within the British establishment, which feared all 'revolutionary' ideas. Having brought the Emperor to his knees at Waterloo in 1815, it would have seemed odd to adopt a monetary system which had its origins in an ideology that it regarded as both alien and dangerous.

With the exception of the two-shilling silver florin, first issued in 1849, worth one tenth of a pound and the double florin, or four-shilling piece, introduced in 1887, which were further small steps towards decimalisation, fundamental change was resisted. The florin survived until 1967, but the double florin failed to gain acceptance and was struck only between 1887 and 1890.

However, in the middle of the 19th century, when the traumas of the Napoleonic wars receded and prosperity grew, the debate about decimalisation emerged again. Although progress was very pedestrian, the Decimalisation Association was founded in 1841 to promote decimalisation and metrication and reflected, by a growing realisation in commerce and industry, the importance of making international trade as straightforward as possible.

Following the 1851 Great Exhibition, there was an awareness of the importance of trade for Britain's growing economic prominence. Shortly afterwards, in a preliminary report issued in 1857, entitled the Royal Commission on Decimal Coinage, the pluses and minuses of decimalisation were considered. However, the report failed to draw any conclusions concerning the introduction of a new currency system. A final report in 1859 from commissioners, Lord Overstone and the Governor of the Bank of England, John Hubbard, decided against the idea of decimalising British currency, claiming that it had 'few merits'.

In 1862, the Select Committee on Weights and Measures reported favourably concerning the introduction of decimalisation to accompany the introduction of metrication and decimalisation.

A summary of its report makes for interesting reading as it contains phrases that resonate to the present day.

> "After full and careful consideration of the evidence, your Committee has arrived at a unanimous conclusion, that the best course to adopt is, cautiously but steadily, to introduce the Metric system into this country.
>
> It therefore recommends:
>
> 1. That the use of the Metric system be rendered legal.
>
> 2. That a Department of Weights and Measures be

Gadgets, such as this analogue conversion tool, were available to consumers in 1971, but often added an extra layer of complexity, rather than simplifying the situation.

established in connection with the Board of Trade, to promote the use, and extend the knowledge of, the Metric system, in the departments of Government, and among the people:

3. The Government should sanction the use of the Metric system in the levying of customs duties; thus, familiarising it among our merchants and manufacturers,

and giving facilities to foreign traders in their dealings with this country:

4. The Metric system should form one of the subjects of examination in the Competitive Examinations of the Civil Service:

5. The gramme should be used as a weight for foreign letters and books at the Post-office:

6. The Committee of Council on Education should require the Metric system to be taught in all schools receiving grants of public money:

7. In the public Statistics of the country quantities should be expressed in terms of the Metric system in juxtaposition with those of our own; as suggested by the International Statistical Congress.

8. In Private Bills before Parliament, the use of the Metric system should be allowed.

9. The only weights and measures in use should be the Metric and Imperial, until the Metric has been generally adopted.

Your Committee feel it to be right to add that the evidence they have received tends to convince them that a decimal system of money should, as nearly as possible, accompany a decimal system of weights and measures. Both the foreign and English witnesses think the maximum of advantage cannot be attained without a combination of the two.

Such is an outline of the course recommended by your

Committee for introducing into this country a system which may tend to enlarge our foreign trade – hitherto imperfectly developed, if not neglected – with countries yearly becoming more and more mutually connected and mutually dependent; most of them composing the great European family of nations, and many of them near our own shores.

Your Committee think that no country, especially no commercial country, should fail to adopt a system which will save time and lessen labour; which will give to trade greater certainty in its operations, diminish the intermediate agency with which it is encumbered, render more exact machine-making, engineering and manufactures, and remove a number of arithmetical barriers which stand, like obstructive toll-bars, on the highway of education. It has been the destiny of this country to lead the way in introducing the great principles of commercial freedom. Let us not reject the use of those implements which may facilitate their application. Most of all, let us rejoice, if, by adopting a system freely and rapidly extending itself, and becoming more and more an international one, we may assist in promoting the peace, and enlarging the commerce, of the world.

15th July 1862"

Despite the report's conclusions, conservative political opposition was significant. For example, William Ewart Gladstone, then Chancellor of the Exchequer, made his views

Opposite: The new decimal five pence was first released in 1968, more than two years before changeover, and was the same size and value as the predecimal shilling, to allow people to become accustomed to the new coins and their values.

very clear, "I cannot doubt that a decimal system would be of immense advantage in money transactions...But I do not think we have obtained sufficient evidence as to the sense and feeling of the country with respect to it. It is, as you are aware, the enormous masses of the community with immense business to transact who must guide the Government in the matter." As a consummate politician, Gladstone was, of course, using what he had decided was the 'view of the people', to justify and reinforce his own opinion.

By the turn of the twentieth century, Britain, its global power and influence at their zenith, still felt it had no need to change its ancient currency. Indeed, many thought that it was the country's time-honoured idiosyncrasies that were at the core of its strength. In researching this book, I came across a fascinating booklet written by Canadian actuary and scientific polymath, Arthur Harvey, and published by Hunter Rose in Toronto in 1901. In his booklet, he covered a vast range of issues and suggestions about numeration and decimalisation, including money, weights and measures and scientific calculations. In his analysis of Britain's currency, he made the following observations.

"The coinage is stable and in accord its system of accounts and decimalisation has to be approached with much caution. The only possible unit there is the present pound sterling. A committee of the House of Commons in 1853 recorded their conviction that the pound sterling must be maintained but thought that obstacles to its decimalisation were 'not of such nature as to create any doubt of the expediency of introducing that system'." He went on to remark that from his Canadian perspective, "to us who have with ease glided into the use of decimal moneys, it seems that the people of Great Britain are unduly conservative, for the changes needed are very simple."

Harvey then suggested, "A nomenclature, merely by way of a respectful suggestion, as follows:

> £1 pound = 10 florins
> 1 florin = 10 dismes
> 1 dismes = 10 doits
> (Disme - from Old French, was a US 10 cent coin
> struck in 1792. Doit – borrowed from Middle
> German, was an old Dutch coin)

He then made a particularly telling point, saying, "The appearance of £43.825 instead of £43/16s/8½d. would not be strange for long." Harvey was right of course, but it took another 70 years before Britain decimalised its currency.

The Great War of 1914 and the pressures it imposed on national finance renewed interest in the decimalisation debate. In July 1916, a 'Committee on Commercial and Industrial Policy after the War' was appointed. It considered, among other things, proposals for the introduction of a decimal system of coinage, submitted by Lord Cunliffe, at that time the Governor of the Bank of England. Cunliffe's proposals were based on gold sovereigns and half sovereigns; silver crowns, florins, and shillings; but also introduced the concept of 'new pence' of which there were to be 200 to the sovereign. The scheme only required, in addition to the existing copper penny 1 (new) pence, halfpenny, half a (new) pence, three new coins: the 5 (new) pence piece equal to 6 (old) pence, a 'dime' equal to 2 (new) pence, and a 'mil' equal to a fifth a (new) pence.

There were many decisions to be made on the path to decimalisation, not just the name of the pound in the decimal era. These very rare test pieces for Britain's decimal coinage (above) show that we may have had 'cents' instead of pence, and that the 50p was initially contemplated as a ten-sided coin. Many other variations occur, such as tests with aluminium and brass, and tests with coins of 5,10, 25 and 50 pence.

The Committee in its Final Report stressed the upheaval which would be caused by decimalisation in the lives of wage earners, retail shopkeepers and their customers and concluded that, "the introduction of such a change would be inexpedient at a time when the social, industrial and financial organisation of the country will be faced with numerous and exceptional difficulties."

In 1920, a Royal Commission on Decimal Coinage chaired by Lord Emmott, the former Liberal MP for Oldham and Director of the War Trade Department from 1915 to 1919, reported that the only feasible scheme was to divide the pound into

1,000 'mills', a system first proposed in 1824, but that it would be too inconvenient to introduce and "not advisable to make any change (formatting)in the denomination of the currency and money of account of the United Kingdom with a view to placing them on a decimal basis." A minority of four members said that the disruption would be worthwhile. A further three members recommended that the pound should be replaced by the 'royal', consisting of 100 halfpennies, with there then being 4.8 royals to the former pound.

Emmott's report effectively disposed of the subject for more than thirty years. Even as late as 1955, an attempt to pass a decimal currency bill through Parliament fell at its second reading. However, there was renewed and growing interest during the late 1950s, which was furthered in 1960 by the publication of a joint report by Committees appointed by the British Association for the Advancement of Science and the Association of British Chambers of Commerce. Significantly, by then the stark facts of life about the decline in Britain's global power and its diminishing status in the world were clear for all to see. Much as it pained them, both the general population and those in power, realised that Britain could no longer cling to its glorious past and all its trappings; its ancient currency among them.

As Churchill had remarked at the end of the Second World War, "There I sat with the great Russian bear on one side of me with paws outstretched, and, on the other side, the great American buffalo. Between the two sat the poor little English donkey." Not only had Britain emerged from the war fundamentally weakened, by the 1960s its once mighty empire was crumbling. It could no longer dictate to commonwealth governments, which all wanted to set their own agendas.

Former British colonies began to modernise their currencies, and in doing so, rejected £.s.d. India decimalised the rupee 16 anna and 64 paise to 100 naya paise in 1957. In South Africa, a 1958 report committed the country to a 10-shilling equivalent unit. There were similar steps in New Zealand, Australia and the Irish Republic. Indeed, Australia contemplated the naming of its new currency, the 'royal', but chose the less imperialistic 'dollar', divided into 'cents'. Before long, Britain's antiquated currency system was shared only by Nigeria, Malta and the Gambia; a very small family on the world stage. Out of step and on the fringe of a European continent rapidly integrating and becoming a more and more important marketplace, Britain had little choice but to change.

In 1961, the then Chancellor of the Exchequer, Mr. Selwyn Lloyd, announced the formation of a Committee of Inquiry under the chairmanship of Lord Halsbury to consider the form which decimalisation might take, its timing and likely cost. Suddenly, it seemed that it was no longer a matter of whether decimalisation was a good idea, but rather, how and when.

As the Chancellor explained, "The Government's view is that real advantage would follow from the adoption of a decimal currency, but the matter must depend a little upon the cost and other relevant considerations. In the light of the findings of the Committee, we will make the final decision." The Bank of England submitted a memorandum to the Committee in April 1962, arguing in favour of retaining the pound as the main unit in any decimal system. This was the recommendation of a majority of the Committee, the Report of which was published in September 1963. The Government adopted the

Mr James Callaghan, then Chancellor of the Exchequer, with members of the Decimal Currency Board. Left to right; Mrs E. M. Dodds, Mr Callaghan, Lord Errol of Hale (Deputy Chairman) and Sir William Fiske (chairman). The Decimal Currency Board was set up to examine problems and to promote the speedy transition to a decimal currency and organised a programme of guidance to the public.

majority view of the Committee, and arrangements were set in train for the introduction of the new system, almost 300 years after Sir William Petty had made his proposals in 1682. The greatest change in British currency in its entire history, at least a millennium, was imminent.

Although Halsbury had reported in 1963, domestic politics got in the way of progress. After thirteen years in power, the Conservative Party, led by Sir Alec Douglas-Home, lost the

October 1964 general election to Harold Wilson's Labour Party by just four seats. It would be a further three years, on 1st March 1966 before the new Labour Chancellor, James Callaghan, made an official announcement to Parliament. He said firmly, "The cost of going decimal is heavy, but you recover it within a year or two and from then on you get a permanent bonus all the way through." Wilson then won a snap election in 1966 by a landslide, which meant that progress towards decimalisation would become part of a reformist Labour agenda until just eight months before D-Day, when it unexpectedly lost the June 1970 general election to Edward Heath's Conservatives.

Although the decision to decimalise had been taken, there was much to be done and many points of detail to be considered, most of which were surrounded by sensitivities and heated debate. Should the major unit of the new currency be based on the pound or the 10-shilling unit? Australia's expression of regret about its choice of 10-shillings was influential, as was the emotive point that the pound sterling was a symbolic part of Britain's heritage. Not surprisingly, the pound won the day.

Then there was the debate about the new secondary unit. Should it be the penny, as it always had been, or should it be a 'cent', in line with many other currencies? Halsbury had preferred the penny and James Callaghan made it crystal clear, tradition should prevail. He called the penny an 'amiable relic', saying, "I much prefer the penny. Why should we go American...The penny is good; it is indeed the oldest coin in Britain. It was originally a silver coin. I see no reason why we should adopt the cent, it's a miserable sounding word by comparison with the penny."

Determined to stick to the original schedule of February 1971,

Harold Wilson pushed forward the necessary legislation in March 1967 and it received Royal Assent on 13th July 1967.

Crucial to the planning was the establishment of a Decimal Currency Board, which had the explicit tasks of:

Examining in detail the problems of the changeover, including, as necessary, consultation with interested parties.

Promoting the speedy and efficient transition to the use of decimal currency.

Organising a programme of guidance for the public.

Examining any claims for compensation and making recommendations thereon.

Lord (Bill) Fiske of Brent, former Labour leader of the Greater London Council chaired the Board, a group made up of people from industry, commerce, retail and trade unions.

While the politicians came and went and the wheels of Parliament turned, the Royal Mint got on with the practicalities. New coins had to be designed, approved and then minted in vast quantities. Even prior to publication of the Halsbury Report various creative organisations were invited to form teams that would compete against one another to produce new decimal designs.

Three groups were formed: The Royal Institute of British Architects, the Royal Academy and a third combined team comprising the Royal College of Art and Royal Designers for Industry. One of the RCA/RDI team's designers, Geoffrey Clarke, produced ideas that were particularly radical.

He proposed coins where all the textual information was restricted to one side. They were thought to be far too extreme and dismissed.

Also from the RCA/RDI team, the artist and coin designer, Christopher Ironside, already well known for many coin designs, produced ideas which were much more appealing, and he was invited to progress them for the decimal reverses. Meanwhile, the Royal Mint Advisory Committee (RMAC) selected Arnold Machin from the Royal Academy to sculpt a new portrait of the Queen. He was granted four sittings with the Queen at Buckingham Palace and a final one at Balmoral. His portrait, which replaced Mary Gillick's coronation portrait, first featured on the new decimal coinage of Australia from 1966.

A first set of reverses was completed by Ironside between 1963 and 1966. Their development was not without difficulty. The design for the 2p, featuring Britannia, was particularly challenging, leading to it being the last to gain approval from the RMAC, prior to being shown to Cabinet ministers in July 1966.

The original trawl for design ideas had included ideas from the general public in Britain, but also from the Commonwealth. Over 900 drawings were received in a spectrum from the highly polished and creative, to the crude and naïve. The British Museum's Curator of Medals and Modern Money, Tom Hockenhull, in his excellent 2021 book 'Making Change' described some of the more entertaining entrants. "A Miss A.I.D. Dennis from Tunbridge Wells managed to squeeze a daffodil, leek, shamrock, thistle, rose, denomination and a portrait of the Queen, all on to one side of her sketch of a 10p piece. Another New Zealand entrant produced an imaginative

Mr Christopher Ironside, creator of the reverse designs of the new decimal coins, examines some of his work in the form of the new 50p coin. His designs came in for criticism at the time as they were very different to the predecimal designs they were replacing. However, in the fullness of time, they have come to be appreciated for the modernising influence they have had, and what was needed at the time, to create a satisfactory break with the past.

landscape featuring St Paul's Cathedral and the recently completed BT Tower but noted that he wasn't sure what the latter landmark looked like. The result would not have looked out of place in a work of science fiction."

The discussion over how to replace the 10-shilling ('10-bob') note became protracted. By the mid-1960s, the average life of the famous 'pink lady' was only five months. Decimalisation

provided an opportunity to replace the note with a coin, which would of course become a 50p piece. There were several suggestions that the new coin should be multi-sided. There was, of course, a precedent, the 'thruppenny bit'; much liked but difficult to produce, which had twelve sides.

50p coins of ten and twelve sides were considered, as was a square coin, which was quickly discarded as impractical. Companies involved in cash-handling were consulted, as were vending machine companies, all of which were less than enthusiastic about anything other than a round coin. Market research was undertaken with cross sections of housewives, who tested a range of coin shapes and sizes. A ten-sided coin was the most popular, but a seven-sided example came a close second. So, after much due diligence, the Decimal Currency Board erred on the side of the vending machine lobby and went for a seven-sided coin, what is, strictly speaking, an equilateral curve heptagon. Patrick O'Leary of the Times could not resist the comment, "It's difficult to get emotional over a piece of cupro-nickel whose shape is officially described as an equilateral curve heptagon."

Finally, after a careful and considered process, the new decimal coinage was ready. With Arnold Machin's new portrait of a strikingly attractive Queen on the obverse of all of them, the five coins were minted in huge quantities:

50p - 19.4 million

10p - 133.5 million

5p - 225.9 million

Opposite: The new decimal two pence was released in 1971 at the time of changeover, although souvenir sets of coins including it had already been on sale to allow people to become accustomed to the new size and design. The decimal 2p was worth 4.8 predecimal pence.

2p - 1,454.8 million

1p - 1.521.6 million

The reverse of the new 1p coin showed a crowned and chained portcullis reminiscent of the House of Beaufort Portcullis adopted by Henry VII and the House of Tudor. The reverse of the 2p coin featured the three ostrich feathers of the Prince of Wales held by a coronet with the motto, ICH DIEN, ('I serve'). The 5p reverse was decorated with Scotland's crowned thistle. The 10p coin displayed England's crowned lion passant. Finally, the 50p coin displayed a rather languorous Britannia. Seated beside a resting lion and her Union shield, she holds a trident in her right hand and an olive branch in her right. The two objects are a little contradictory, but that's heraldry for you!

The enormous demand for coinage for decimalisation, at least four billion coins, would put a significant strain on the Royal Mint's somewhat antiquated facilities on Tower Hill in London. The construction of the Tower Hill Mint had been started in 1805 and was completed by 1809. The site was fronted by the imposing Johnson Smirke Building, named after its designer James Johnson and its builder Robert Smirke. On both sides of the building were gatehouses behind which buildings housed the mint's new machinery. The entire site was protected by a boundary wall patrolled by the Royal Mint's military guard.

During World War II, the Tower Mint played a vital role in ensuring that people were paid for their services with hard currency rather than banknotes. Over the course of the war

Opposite: Drums of shiny new 'coppers', just some of the thousands-of-millions of new coins being minted and stockpiled at the Royal Mint in Wales, in preparation for D-Day in 1971.

the Royal Mint was hit on several occasions, and at one point was put out of commission for three weeks. As technology changed with the introduction of electricity and demand continued to grow, the process of rebuilding continued so that by the 1960s little of the original mint remained, apart from Smirke's 1809 building and its gatehouses at the front.

When the government announced the plans to decimalise our currency it was starkly obvious that Tower Hill would be unable to meet the demands of the recoinage and that a new mint was needed. Over twenty sites were considered. However, the small Welsh town of Llantrisant, ten miles northwest of Cardiff, was eventually chosen. Work began in August 1967 with the first phase of the mint formally opened in December 1968. The second phase of construction began in 1973. Upon completion the final cost for the land, buildings and plant came to £8 million. Coin minting gradually shifted to the new site over the next seven years, and the last coin, a gold sovereign, was struck in London in November 1975.

The Tower Hill site was the subject of several planning proposals over the years, including a major office and leisure complex. However, the current situation has involved a sale to China for a new Chinese embassy, which is currently going through the planning process.

One of the main tasks of the Decimal Currency Board prior to D-Day was to organise a publicity and advertising campaign to provide information to commerce, industry and the public and also to try to allay the misgivings about the transition, which were of course commonplace. The DCB decided on a three-tier approach. The first was a focus on the new coinage, the second emphasised the impact on retail and prices and the third on how the comparisons between the old and the

Chairman of the Decimal Currency Board, William Fiske, shows a guide published by the Board to assist consumers with the changeover. Publicity and advertising became very intense as the February 1971 deadline approached.

new could be best understood by users.

All forms of media were used in a 'Countdown to D-Day' format, which became particularly intense in late 1970. Decimalisation messaging even made its way into popular television programmes of the time, like Coronation Street and The Archers, while Steptoe and Son's Wilfred Brambell and

singer/comedian Max Bygraves both released songs to mark decimalisation.

'Decimal Conversion' devices of all sorts were manufactured to help people understand the new currency and to make calculations. Some were helpful but most were less so and in the main an attempt to cash-in on public uncertainty and anxiety. There were 'decimal adders' with push buttons and 'decimal currency convertors' with rotating plastic discs which revealed old and new amounts when moved in sequence. Board game manufacturers soon released a range of games with 'decimal' themes like Waddington's 'Sum it' and there was also an avalanche of memorabilia of all kinds, including the usual mugs and tea towels.

Despite all the government planning and the careful preparations of the DCB, there would be a sting in the tail for the decimalisation process. It came in the form of a small, low value coin that quickly took on huge significance. It was the much-loved sixpence, the 'tanner', that caused the greatest stir. If the 10-shilling base had been chosen for decimalisation, the sixpence, as a 5-cent coin, would have been fine, but under a pound system, it was worth 2½p, far less appropriate. So, under the 1969 Decimal Currency Act, the sixpence was to be abolished.

The sixpence was a very useful pre-decimalisation coin, particularly for vending, parking and similar coin-operated machines. Just to confuse matters, after the Currency Act left the Commons and went to the Lords, their lordships

Opposite: The new decimal penny was released in 1971 at the time of changeover, although souvenir sets of coins including it had already been on sale to allow people to become accustomed to the new size and design. The decimal 1p was worth 2.4 predecimal pence.

DECIMAL
CURRENCY
BOARD
When you go
decimal shopping,
remember
10/- = 50p
2/- = 10p
1/- = 5p
So sixpence equals 2½p

passed an amendment putting the sixpence back in, only for the Commons to reverse it again! Consequently, the press, ever-hungry for a good story, launched a 'Save our Sixpence' campaign, largely based on the common view that the new low-denomination coins would lead to prices being rounded up rather than rounded down. The prestigious Financial Times waded in on behalf of the sixpence. Lombard, the British business column wrote, "Anyone who thinks about it for more than a few minutes will have no difficulty in seeing that the case for allowing the sixpence to live in our decimalised currency is well-nigh irresistible."

The campaigners were soon called 'Tanner Crusaders', who, led by the Evening Standard, were particularly vociferous in London where tube and bus fares were largely based on the sixpence coin. Typically, rather than stick to their guns, the politicians sensed that they could curry favour with the public by appearing to be flexible and able to listen to the public's concerns. So, in April 1970, Chancellor of the Exchequer, Roy Jenkins, announced that the sixpence would be saved at 2½p for at least two years. It was not only a piece of political opportunism, it was also clever, because rising prices soon diminished the value of the coin; so much so, that when the little 'tanner' was finally withdrawn in 1980, under Margaret Thatcher's administration, there were only a handful of letters of complaint.

Interestingly, in 2016, the Royal Mint began minting legal tender decimal sixpence coins in silver. They were intended to

Opposite: The sixpence, which should have been left behind at the time of changeover, pushed its way into the decimal era as this banner, displayed by William Fiske, shows. Note the very bottom line on the banner. The sixpence was subject to a 'remain crusade' campaign and as a result retained its legal tender status until 1980.

be bought as Christmas presents. They were heavier than the pre-1970 sixpences (3.35 grams instead of 2.83 grams) and had a denomination of six new pence rather six old pence. .

By far the most onerous part of decimalisation was the huge undertaking required within industry and commerce to make sure their various functions and systems were ready for D-Day. It was, in fact, a national mobilisation on a vast scale. Of course, computer-based systems were in their infancy in the late sixties, so much of the work had to be done manually.

An illustration of the scale of the task is provided by some examples of the number of business machines and coin operated machines in use in Britain in 1968:

Business Machines
Adding 750,000
Accounting 100,000
Calculating 60,000
Cash Registers 616,000
Ticket machines 100,000
Taximeters 27,000

Coin-operated Machines
Vending of all kinds (service & commodity) 1,750,000
Gas & Electricity meters 400,000
Post office machines 260,500
Amusement & Gaming 350,000

The numbers speak for themselves and are a stark illustration of what needed to be done over the planning period for D-Day. The fact that it was done with significant success is a

Ensuring the new coins would work with the millions of ticket and other business machines at the time was a large part of the Decimal Currency Board's function. Here, William Fiske, Chairman of the Board is at London's Euston Station trying the new Automatic Ticketing Machines.

testament to the efficiency of British industry and commerce at the time. It is difficult to estimate the total cost of the exercise, but the DCB's original estimate of £100m may well have been fairly accurate. It is worth noting that £100m in 1971 is now worth about £1.4 billion today.

I am indebted to Tom Hockenhull's excellent 2021 book, Making Change* for three accounts that capture the human dimension of decimalisation. In 1970, Tony McMahon was a junior clerk at the Federated Employers Insurance Company. He was presented with several large ledgers of claims with figures in £.s.d., which all had to be converted to decimal. "There was no calculator, but it was assumed that as I had just left school with 'O level' maths, I was ideally suited. I'm not sure how long it took me, but I was still doing it on February 15th, 1971!"

Reg Holmes worked for a chartered accountancy firm in London, where he had to update all the company's balances into decimals. "The net result was that by December 1970, I had done so many conversions I could do them in my head without thinking about them. I became very popular for weeks after February 15th. As others fiddled with their conversion charts, I could tell them the amounts straight away."

John Miller was employed by a solicitors' office in Edinburgh. "I hated doing the accounts. It was a tedious job at the best of times, but to track every transaction to the exact penny, not only doubled the work, but also threw up discrepancies where old money would not convert exactly into new. The resulting compromises, whilst of no real financial consequence, hastened the end of that kind of accounting and introduced the world of 'near enough' – thank goodness!"

The Sainsbury supermarket chain, at that time the country's leading grocery retailer, proved to be a model example of decimalisation preparation. The company wanted to do everything it could to enable the change to be as smooth as possible for both its customers and its staff. As a consequence, it came up with a creative initiative.

* _Making Change_ Tom Hockenhull, Spink Books/British Museum 2021, p 63

Over a year before D-Day, on 10th February 1970, Sainsbury's opened the first 'Decimal Shop' in Britain. This was housed at 9/11 London Road, Croydon. It was a branch with a distinguished Sainsbury's pedigree: the first suburban branch to be opened, the first to have Sainsbury's House Style design introduced to the interior and exterior and the first to be converted to self-service. Earmarked for closure, the company's board decided that, before its demise, it would be the ideal location for an experiment in new decimal currency. The branch was re-modelled with both a model decimal currency counter service and a self-service area in which shopping could be tried out in the new currency. Please note, self-service shops were still relatively new in 1970.

The motivation for the experiment was the training of staff. Managers and other staff, including a new Decimal Training Officer for each shop, could get real-life exposure to the new currency, which they could then use back in their own branches. Sainsbury's was also keen to see how real customers responded to the new coins and system.

Fears about hidden (rounding up) price rises during the conversion were a real concern for the general public and Sainsbury's made a specific commitment that on D-Day it would round down prices rather than round up. At the demonstration shop, the prices were converted at the official rate, but when it came to D-Day, Sainsbury's did indeed make sufficient price reductions on the conversion to honour its guarantee that the customer was overall better off on the new decimal prices than the old prices.

Staff training was, of course, the biggest challenge for any retailer in going decimal, but it was by no means the only one. For example, Sainsbury's had the problem of converting

its equipment, which included over 3,000 cash registers and approximately 1,500 scales, not to mention the office and accounting systems across its business. Sainsbury's decimal shop was open until November 1970, during which over 30,000 shoppers and 1500 staff got a preview of decimal shopping, which meant that it was very well prepared for D-Day itself.

Schools and education were also important areas of concern for the DCB. At the time, Britain had a relatively decentralised education and curriculum regime. So, in consultation with the Department of Education and Science, the DCB was restricted to acting in an advisory capacity with the Schools Council on guidance material which the Council might issue. For example, the best-selling teaching guide, Change for a Pound, produced by the Council's Mathematics Committee in 1969, offered factual information for teachers and children alike.

Other organisations, like the Banking Education Service and the National Savings Committee, provided support material like wallcharts for classrooms. Also, free booklets, one entitled, Expression of amounts in printing, writing and in speech (March 1968) and one with the title, Britain's new coins, (September 1968) were sent to every school, but only one copy per school. Given the scale of the change to Britain's society represented by decimal changeover, these provisions for schools seem a little haphazard and inadequate.

The new facility of the Royal Mint in south Wales with stockpiles of new decimal coins worth more than five million pounds, in readiness for decimal changeover.

1971 ARRIVES

1971 began inauspiciously, when on 2nd January, 66 people died on a stairway at the Rangers - Celtic football match at Ibrox. The next day saw the beginning of the Open University, while two days later, the cricket revolution began when the first One Day international cricket match was played between Australia and England at the Melbourne Cricket Ground. There was unwelcome news on 4th February, when it was announced that Rolls Royce had gone bankrupt. However, it was immediately nationalised as the government-owned 'Rolls-Royce Limited'.

There were two events of significance in Africa in January. On the 15th, the Aswan High Dam opened in Egypt and on the 25th, in Uganda, Idi Amin deposed Milton Obote in a coup to become the country's new president, an office he would hold in a brutal regime until he was deposed in 1979.

The big stories in America were the guilty verdict in the trial of Charles Manson and his 'family' for the 1969 murders of actress Sharon Tate and her guests and the launch of Apollo 14, which landed on the Moon on 5th February.

Elsewhere, the government of Poland announced that it was reversing the increase of food prices that had triggered

Opposite: The new decimal half penny was released in 1971 and was unpopular from the moment it was released. It was small, easily lost, and had virtually no purchasing power. It was worth 1.2 predecimal pence.

nationwide rioting in December, and that prices would return to normal on 1st March. At the same time, Prime Minister, Piotr Jaroszewicz, announced that plans to raise wages would be halted as a compromise for the reduction of food prices.

In Belgium, anger over proposed price increases for agricultural supplies proposed by the European Economic Community's Agricultural Commissioner, led a group of Belgian farmers to bring three cows into a meeting room in

William Fiske, Chairman of the Decimal Currency Board visits a chain-store in London's Edgware Road after closing time. Cash registers and ticketing then changed over to decimal currency, and here Mr Fiske assists in changing over the price tickets.

Brussels, where the six EEC nations' ministers of agriculture were meeting to discuss pricing. A reporter noted that the stunt was "a major feat of cowherding" in that they "had succeeded in driving three cows... through swift swing doors, past security guards, up three flights of marble steps, through a press room, down a corridor and into the council chamber." France's Minister of Agriculture commented that, "It was an event unworthy of the concept of Europe."

For those of us familiar with our more liberal times, perhaps the most surprising story from early 1971 came from Switzerland on 7th February. Following a national referendum women were granted the right to vote in state elections. However, women's suffrage did not extend to many Swiss cantons, the last of which, Appenzell Innerhoden, did not grant the right until 1991 and only when forced to do so by the victory of two women from the canton, who took their case to Switzerland's federal court.

The Irish Republic also converted its currency to decimal on February 15th, allowing Ireland and the UK's Northern Ireland to have a similar system. In addition to Ireland, the African nation of Malawi went decimal on the same day, along with Gibraltar.

Monday 15th February, D-Day itself, was a dull and damp day across London and the south, but much brighter in the north and west. Ted Heath was prime minister, and George Harrison's My Sweet Lord was number one in the pop charts. The banks had been closed since the end of the previous Wednesday so that they could complete what was called, 'The single biggest operation in the history of British banking'. Most importantly, the banks were required to clear all cheques in pre-decimal amounts in a task dubbed 'Operation Checkpoint'. The Royal

Bank of Scotland took the exercise particularly seriously. Its head office kept its staff canteen open for 24 hours over the entire four days to keep its staff going.

Harrods took to D-Day with the somewhat flamboyant gesture of creating 'Decimal Penny' advisers. Dressed very noticeably in straw boaters with bright blue sashes, each department had an attractive young woman to, 'deal with all queries, difficulties, or any out of the way problems which may arise'. Fittingly, they were there in numbers, surrounded by a posse of reporters, photographers and cameramen when the DCB chairman, Bill Fiske visited the store on St Valentine's Day.

The period after D-Day could accurately be described as a honeymoon period. Apart from a few minor wrinkles and a modicum of sensationalism in the press, the great monetary conversion had gone well. A female journalist for the Daily Express wrote in late February, "I'm all for the new slimline currency. For the first time in my life, there is actually room for my purse in my bag. For the first time ever, I can store a spot of ready cash in a coat pocket without wrecking its line."

The DCB welcomed investigations into prices to assess whether decimalisation had had an adverse impact on food prices in particular. The Consumer Association conducted a survey in each of the two weeks before the transition and for five weeks afterwards. Its subsequent report to the DCB came to the following conclusions:

Opposite: retailers sought to help customers in many different ways. Harrods of London trained 75 women as 'Decimal Pennies' to roam the store and assist with decimal conversion. Here they are seem with William Fiske, Decimal Currency Board Chairman, who had visited the retailer to see last minute conversions of cash registers and goods being price-marked in the new currency.

On the whole, retailers stuck to the 'Shoppers Guide', when rounding up and rounding down.

Although there has been a gradual drift upwards of prices during the seven weeks of the survey, it is hard to separate the normal inflationary trend from a possible decimalisation trend.

It does appear that shopkeepers and shop assistants are handling the new currency quite well. For example, in spot checks in the two weeks before the changeover, 16 out of 26 bills were wrong, while in the final two weeks of the survey (weeks 6 and 7) only 5 out of 26 were wrong.

The Daily Sketch offered a more succinct summary. "Four weeks ago Britain went decimal, with a forecast that this would send prices soaring. Well, here's the good news. It hasn't."

By March 1971, the most significant news was the extent to which the practical benefits of the changeover were beginning to be seen across the economy. Several different parts of industry and commerce, notably those involving accounting, bookkeeping, computing and all areas related to banking, reported greater efficiencies and cost savings. The pace of change had exceeded the DCB's expectations. For example, the Automatic Vending Association of Britain reported that 95% of machines had been converted by the end of March. Similarly, the Post Office reported that 99% of telephone

Opposite: one of the many press ads placed by the Decimal Currency Board to popularise the new decimal coins.

Overleaf: One of the busiest parts of Lewis's Department Store in Manchester City Centre on the 15th February 1971, is the 'banking section' which is changing over old coins for new decimal currency.

A simple guide to our new money

Next year, on Monday, 15th February 1971, three new coins will join the money at present in your purse, and Britain's new money system will have started.

This simple guide will help you to understand our new money. Nearer D (for Decimal) Day, the Decimal Currency Board will be giving full details of the change, including delivery to every home in Britain of **a free illustrated booklet.** This will include advice on shopping with the new money. By the time we change, everyone will be quite familiar with our decimal coinage.

The £ stays the same

In our new money system, the £ note does not change in any way. It will still be called £1 and will have 'one pound' written on it. We shall use the £ note just as we do now, and, of course, the same is true of the £5 note and the £10 note.

We are already using all the 'silver' coins

Open your purse and look at the 'silver.' You may have a 50p (which you are using as 10 shillings), a two shilling piece (which may have either 'two shillings' or '10 new pence' on it) and a shilling (which may have either 'one shilling' or '5 new pence' on it). All these are in use now and all of them continue.

So **fifty new pence** in new money is ten shillings in the old. **Ten new pence** in new money is two shillings in the old. **Five new pence** in new money is a shilling in the old. And we know them all already.

Now meet our handy new 'coppers'

These three coins, the 'coppers' (which have '2 new pence,' '1 new penny' and '½ new penny' written on them) are the only coins that will actually be new on D (for Decimal) Day. See how handy they are; much smaller and lighter than the old penny.

With our new money there will be **100 new pence in each £** instead of 12 pennies to the shilling and 20 shillings to the pound. So, although it is smaller and lighter, remember that one new penny (1p) will be worth more than 2d in the old money.

The threepenny bit and the old penny can be used, at most, for 18 months after D Day. The sixpence will remain for at least two years.

15th February 1971 is the day we change to decimal money

CHANGE YOUR OLD COPPER

LEWIS'S BANK
DECIMAL CHANGE & ENQUIRIES
IN ORDER TO MAKE FOR SPEEDY
SERVICE. CUSTOMERS ARE REQUESTED
TO CHANGE THEIR OLD
FOR NEW PENCE.

Approaches to customer assistance varied widely. This publicity shot shows a 'Decimal Dolly' in hot pants, at the Trustee Savings Bank, assisting a customer with his enquiry.

coin-boxes had been converted within four weeks of D-Day.

Dual-pricing in shops was widely abandoned before the end of March, by which time old pennies and threepenny bits had all but disappeared from circulation. Tellingly, the Daily Mirror leader article of 24th March proclaimed, "Nobody wanted decimal currency, just no one wanted the 10-bob bit, now that it's here we don't know how we managed without it."

By June of 1971, 'decimalisation' was no longer a topic appearing in the newspapers. Parliament was silent on the subject and public contact with the DCB had reduced significantly. In December of 1970, the Board had been receiving an average of 600 letters and 600 telephone calls every week. In January 1971, contacts by telephone rose to 1,000 per week. However, in March the weekly averages were 230 letters and 220 telephone calls, which fell to 140 and 110 respectively by June. Over half the Board's staff of 51 employed on D-Day had gone by the end of March and by the end of June, only 17 were left.

When, on 28th June the Board finally recommended the official end of the changeover period would be 31st August, the then Chancellor of the Exchequer, Anthony Barber, wrote to Bill Fiske, "Now that the end of the Board's task is in sight, I would like to take this opportunity to pay tribute to the way in which it has carried out its function. Naturally enough, the transition from one currency to another has not been without its problems, but from the very first day of the changeover everything has proceeded smoothly, and this is in large measure due to the detailed preparations made by your Board. I should like all members of the Board and the staff to know how much I appreciate all that they have done."

If converting to decimal in the shops was all too much, you could get some practise in with this board game, by Turner Research.

Decimalisation came back into the media spotlight and public consciousness for the final time in August 1971, when the DCB ran its final publicity campaign to announce the imminent end of the changeover period. In particular, it offered the clear warning that 'old pennies' and 'thruppenny bits' were to be de-monetised. "After August 31st, old pennies and 3d bits cannot be used as money: the Board would like to thank the public and business community for their cooperation and understanding, which led to such a smooth changeover." Although the Board's expression of gratitude was distinctly self-congratulatory, it clearly felt entitled to praise itself. No one demurred.

For most people, the biggest challenge after D-Day was how to convert the new decimal prices into the real values that they understood from the prices in old money. For example, one young boy, whose passion was collecting Dinky toy cars reported, "My obsession was collecting toy cars, especially Dinky cars, which were quite expensive. When I went to buy my first one, it was priced at 37.5p in decimal currency, which didn't seem like much. It was only when I did the arithmetic in my head, did I realise the price in old money. I thought, 'Gosh! That's 8 shillings in old money."

I must confess that even now, fifty years after decimalisation, like the Dinky toy collector, I still make small old/new currency calculations. When, as a young man, I first came across the temptations of beer, a cheap pint was about 1 shilling and 10 pence, which in today's decimal money is 9p. However, in 2021, a cheap pint is about £3.80, depending on where you live. When I convert the numbers the other way around, from decimal to old money, my jaw drops; that's a 42-fold increase! To be fair, the escalation in price is a result of inflation and the fall in the buying power of the pound, rather than as a result of decimalisation.

How times have changed!

ABOUT THE AUTHOR

Stewart Binns is a former academic, soldier and teacher and now an author and documentary-maker. After training at the BBC and working on Panorama, he joined Mark McCormack's TWI in 1986. His television credits there include the 'In-Colour' genre of programmes, notably the BAFTA and Grierson winner, 'Britain at War' and the Peabody winner, 'Second World War in Colour'. He also launched Trans World Sport in 1987, Futbol Mundial in 1993, the Olympic Games Camera of Record in 1994 and the Olympic Television Archive Bureau in 1996. Other productions include Century  (1998), Churchill (2003), Tiger, The Official Biography (2004) and Chasing Churchill (2006). He is currently Chief Executive of an independent production company, Big Ape Media International.

His writing credits include non-fiction titles 'The Greatest, Who is Britain's Top Sports Star?' (Boxtree 1996), 'The Second World War in Colour' (Pavilion 1999), 'Britain at War in Colour' (Carlton 2000), 'America at War in Colour' (Carlton 2001) and 'British Empire in Colour' (Carlton 2002).

His first novel, 'Conquest', was published by Penguin in 2011, its sequel, 'Crusade', was released in 2012, the third in the series, 'Anarchy', also in 2013 and the fourth, 'Lionheart', in November 2013. He then focused on the Great War. His first novel, 'Shadow of War' was released in 2014 and its sequel, 'The Darkness and the Thunder' in 2015. His latest book, 'Betrayal', set during The Troubles in Belfast in the early 1980s was released in 2018. Stewart has also authored a number of factual historical books for Hattons of London.

Stewart's home is in Somerset, where he lives with his wife Lucy and twin boys, Charlie and Jack.